Tot's Problem

By Sally Cowan

One night at sunset, Tot stretched out her leg and kicked Patch.

She didn't mean to, but there was no room in the den!

"Look out, Tot!" said Big Jag. "You know what will happen if you wake Patch."

"He'll want to play fight," sighed Tot.

"I'm going out for a snack," said Tot. "Patch will sleep better if I am absent for a while."

She did a big stretch.

Tot jumped up on a tree branch.

She had a big, yellow insect in her sights!

All of a sudden, Chad jumped up.

Chad gave the insect a fright, and it buzzed off!

“That insect was my snack!”
cried Tot.
“I almost caught it!”

Tot sighed.

“You seem upset, Tot,” said Chad. “What’s the problem?”

“Our den is too small for me, Mum and Patch,” said Tot.

I think it's time
to get my own den.
But Mum might object.
She and Patch will miss you!

Tot got home at sunrise.

Patch was awake.
He leaped onto Tot's back!

Tot and Patch rolled around outside the den.

Tot was sleepy, so the play fight was quick!

She did a **big** yawn.

“I taught you a lesson!” cried Patch.

“Patch is so big now, Mum,”
said Tot.
“I should get my own den.”

“That is sudden, but it had to happen one day,” said Big Jag.
“You are such a big girl now, Tot.”

“We’ll miss you so much!”
said Patch.

Goodbye, Tot!
I'll come back for play fights!

CHECKING FOR MEANING

1. Who frightened the insect away? *(Literal)*
2. Why was Tot's play fight with Patch over quickly? *(Literal)*
3. How does Patch feel about Tot? How do you know? *(Inferential)*
4. What are some positive feelings Tot might have about leaving home? What are some less positive feelings she might have? *(Evaluative)*

EXTENDING VOCABULARY

in her sights	What does it mean when Tot had an insect *in her sights*? What verb is related to the word *sights*? How does it help you to understand how *sights* is used in the story?
upset	What is the meaning of the word *upset*? What is another word the author could have used to describe a similar feeling?
object	What might have happened if Big Jag had objected to Tot finding her own den?

MOVING BEYOND THE TEXT

1. Do you have to share a room with a brother or sister? What are (or might be) the problems with sharing a room?
2. How was Chad a good friend to Tot? What can you do to be a good friend to others?
3. Tot and Patch like to play together. What games do you like to play? What game is good for small spaces?
4. Has someone ever objected to something you wanted to do? What did you do then?

TIME TO WRITE

Write about Tot's search for a den of her own. What kind of den does she want? Where would it be?